mountains

A GUIDED JOURNAL THROUGH SCRIPTURE

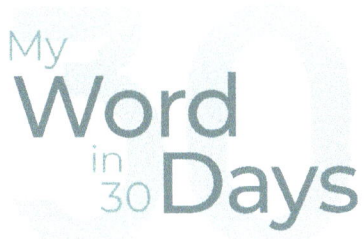

My Word in 30 Days

LYNDSEY LINDSAY

COPYRIGHT ©2022 HILLSEED JOURNALS.
All rights reserved. No part of this book may be reproduced in any form without written permission from the publisher. Do not replicate or copy.

ISBN 978-1-7377809-0-8

Scripture quotations taken from the (NASB®) New American Standard Bible®, Copyright ©1960, 1971, 1977, 1995, 2020 by The Lockman Foundation. Used by permission. All rights reserved. www.lockman.org

Image page 4 by f11photo. Image used under license from Shutterstock.com.
Image page 10 by Ryan DeBerardinis. Image used under license from Shutterstock.com.
Image page 72 by Evgeny Bakharev. Image used under license from Shutterstock.com.

Copyright ©2011 The Montserrat Project Authors (https://github.com/JulietaUla/Montserrat). Used with permission.

Edited by Paula Robertson

Book cover design by The Book Cover Whisperer: ProfessionalBookCoverDesign.com

www.hillseedjournals.com

HOW TO USE THIS JOURNAL

We are so glad you are here!

The Bible is our most useful tool for getting to know who God is and His purpose for our lives, and we can't wait for you to do both.

The pages ahead are grouped into **three parts**, all designed to gently guide you through scripture and prompt you to **pursue the Holy Spirit in this journey over the next 30 days**.

1 Introduction..5

   Start by uncovering your big picture thoughts and ideas for the 30 days ahead that you will spend in scripture.

   You will also find a resource to introduce you to the major themes of the books of the Bible.

2 My Word in 30 Days..11

   Each day will introduce new scripture with consistent and guided journaling prompts.

3 Insights + Action...73

   After digging into *My Word in 30 Days*, you'll put it all together to uncover key biblical insights and faith-based action steps.

Let's grow our understanding of the Bible one day at a time.

For more information and resources:
visit **www.hillseedjournals.com**

introduction

All Scripture is inspired by God and beneficial for teaching, for rebuke, for correction, for training in righteousness; so that the man or woman of God may be fully capable, equipped for every good work.

2 TIMOTHY 3:16–17

Mountains are woven in God's story as a powerful symbol and landscape throughout the Old and New Testaments.

Over the next 30 days, you will explore how mountains appear throughout scripture—from Noah's Ark first finding land after the flood, to Moses climbing seemingly impossible mountains during 40 years in the wilderness, to Jesus' transformational delivery of the Sermon on the Mount.

No matter where you are in your faith, we have all experienced times when we open our Bibles and are unsure of where to start or had difficulty understanding scripture.

This is more than a Bible study. This is more than mountains.

This is about creating confidence to read, reflect, and apply the Word to our lives every day.

MOUNTAINS

What do mountains mean to you? Define the full meaning of mountains in your own words.

What do you want to learn about mountains over the next 30 days? Share your thoughts and ideas below.

RESOURCE | OLD TESTAMENT BOOK THEMES

LAW
Genesis
Exodus
Leviticus
Numbers
Deuteronomy

HISTORY
Joshua
Judges
Ruth
1 Samuel
2 Samuel
1 Kings
2 Kings
1 Chronicles
2 Chronicles
Ezra
Nehemiah
Esther

WISDOM
Job
Psalms
Proverbs
Ecclesiates
Song of Solomon

PROPHECY
Isaiah
Jeremiah
Lamentations
Ezekiel
Daniel
Hosea
Joel
Amos
Obadiah
Jonah
Micah
Nahum
Habakkuk
Zephaniah
Haggai
Zachariah
Malachi

NEW TESTAMENT BOOK THEMES

GOSPELS
Matthew
Mark
Luke
John

HISTORY
Acts

LETTERS
Romans
1 Corinthians
2 Corinthians
Galatians
Ephesians
Philippians
Colossians
1 Thessalonians
2 Thessalonians
1 Timothy
2 Timothy
Titus
Philemon
Hebrews
James
1 Peter
2 Peter
1 John
2 John
3 John
Jude

PROPHECY
Revelation

> **TIP**: *Use this resource to consider the major themes and context of the books of the Bible.*

my word in 30 days

Your word is a lamp to my feet
and a light to my path.

PSALM 119:105

DAY 1 | MOUNTAINS

Pray over today's scripture, asking the Holy Spirit to lead you. Reread it and write what stands out in the space below.

PSALM 125

Observe the text for context, teaching, and themes.

What is God revealing to you?

How can you apply this to your life today?

Prayer + Notes

DAY 2 | MOUNTAINS

Pray over today's scripture, asking the Holy Spirit to lead you. Reread it and write what stands out in the space below.

GENESIS 8

Observe the text for context, teaching, and themes.

What is God revealing to you?

How can you apply this to your life today?

Prayer + Notes

DAY 3 | MOUNTAINS

Pray over today's scripture, asking the Holy Spirit to lead you. Reread it and write what stands out in the space below.

GENESIS 22:1–18

Observe the text for context, teaching, and themes.

What is God revealing to you?

How can you apply this to your life today?

Prayer + Notes

DAY 4 | MOUNTAINS

Pray over today's scripture, asking the Holy Spirit to lead you. Reread it and write what stands out in the space below.

EXODUS 19:1–17

Observe the text for context, teaching, and themes.

What is God revealing to you?

How can you apply this to your life today?

Prayer + Notes

DAY 5 | MOUNTAINS

Pray over today's scripture, asking the Holy Spirit to lead you. Reread it and write what stands out in the space below.

DEUTERONOMY 34

Observe the text for context, teaching, and themes.

What is God revealing to you?

How can you apply this to your life today?

Prayer + Notes

DAY 6 | MOUNTAINS

Pray over today's scripture, asking the Holy Spirit to lead you. Reread it and write what stands out in the space below.

1 KINGS 18:20–39

Observe the text for context, teaching, and themes.

What is God revealing to you?

How can you apply this to your life today?

Prayer + Notes

DAY 7 | MOUNTAINS

Pray over today's scripture, asking the Holy Spirit to lead you. Reread it and write what stands out in the space below.

1 KINGS 19

Observe the text for context, teaching, and themes.

What is God revealing to you?

How can you apply this to your life today?

Prayer + Notes

DAY 8 | MOUNTAINS

Pray over today's scripture, asking the Holy Spirit to lead you. Reread it and write what stands out in the space below.

PSALM 48

Observe the text for context, teaching, and themes.

What is God revealing to you?

How can you apply this to your life today?

Prayer + Notes

DAY 9 | MOUNTAINS

Pray over today's scripture, asking the Holy Spirit to lead you. Reread it and write what stands out in the space below.

ISAIAH 2:1–5

Observe the text for context, teaching, and themes.

What is God revealing to you?

How can you apply this to your life today?

Prayer + Notes

DAY 10 | MOUNTAINS

Pray over today's scripture, asking the Holy Spirit to lead you. Reread it and write what stands out in the space below.

ISAIAH 52:1–12

Observe the text for context, teaching, and themes.

What is God revealing to you?

How can you apply this to your life today?

Prayer + Notes

DAY 11 | MOUNTAINS

Pray over today's scripture, asking the Holy Spirit to lead you. Reread it and write what stands out in the space below.

JEREMIAH 50:3–7

Observe the text for context, teaching, and themes.

What is God revealing to you?

How can you apply this to your life today?

Prayer + Notes

DAY 12 | MOUNTAINS

Pray over today's scripture, asking the Holy Spirit to lead you. Reread it and write what stands out in the space below.

PSALM 68:15–19

Observe the text for context, teaching, and themes.

What is God revealing to you?

How can you apply this to your life today?

Prayer + Notes

DAY 13 | MOUNTAINS

Pray over today's scripture, asking the Holy Spirit to lead you. Reread it and write what stands out in the space below.

EZEKIEL 36

Observe the text for context, teaching, and themes.

What is God revealing to you?

How can you apply this to your life today?

Prayer + Notes

DAY 14 | MOUNTAINS

Pray over today's scripture, asking the Holy Spirit to lead you. Reread it and write what stands out in the space below.

PSALM 95:1–5

Observe the text for context, teaching, and themes.

What is God revealing to you?

How can you apply this to your life today?

Prayer + Notes

DAY 15 | MOUNTAINS

Pray over today's scripture, asking the Holy Spirit to lead you. Reread it and write what stands out in the space below.

MICAH 4:1–8

Observe the text for context, teaching, and themes.

What is God revealing to you?

How can you apply this to your life today?

Prayer + Notes

DAY 16 | MOUNTAINS

Pray over today's scripture, asking the Holy Spirit to lead you. Reread it and write what stands out in the space below.

PSALM 104:5–13

Observe the text for context, teaching, and themes.

What is God revealing to you?

How can you apply this to your life today?

Prayer + Notes

DAY 17 | MOUNTAINS

Pray over today's scripture, asking the Holy Spirit to lead you. Reread it and write what stands out in the space below.

HABAKKUK 3

Observe the text for context, teaching, and themes.

What is God revealing to you?

How can you apply this to your life today?

Prayer + Notes

DAY 18 | MOUNTAINS

Pray over today's scripture, asking the Holy Spirit to lead you. Reread it and write what stands out in the space below.

LUKE 6:12–19

Observe the text for context, teaching, and themes.

What is God revealing to you?

How can you apply this to your life today?

Prayer + Notes

DAY 19 | MOUNTAINS

Pray over today's scripture, asking the Holy Spirit to lead you. Reread it and write what stands out in the space below.

MATTHEW 5–7

Observe the text for context, teaching, and themes.

What is God revealing to you?

How can you apply this to your life today?

Prayer + Notes

DAY 20 | MOUNTAINS

Pray over today's scripture, asking the Holy Spirit to lead you. Reread it and write what stands out in the space below.

JOHN 6:1–14

Observe the text for context, teaching, and themes.

What is God revealing to you?

How can you apply this to your life today?

Prayer + Notes

DAY 21 | MOUNTAINS

Pray over today's scripture, asking the Holy Spirit to lead you. Reread it and write what stands out in the space below.

MARK 11:22–26

Observe the text for context, teaching, and themes.

What is God revealing to you?

How can you apply this to your life today?

Prayer + Notes

DAY 22 | MOUNTAINS

Pray over today's scripture, asking the Holy Spirit to lead you. Reread it and write what stands out in the space below.

MATTHEW 14:22–36

Observe the text for context, teaching, and themes.

What is God revealing to you?

How can you apply this to your life today?

Prayer + Notes

DAY 23 | MOUNTAINS

Pray over today's scripture, asking the Holy Spirit to lead you. Reread it and write what stands out in the space below.

MATTHEW 17:1–13

Observe the text for context, teaching, and themes.

What is God revealing to you?

How can you apply this to your life today?

Prayer + Notes

DAY 24 | MOUNTAINS

Pray over today's scripture, asking the Holy Spirit to lead you. Reread it and write what stands out in the space below.

LUKE 19:28–44

Observe the text for context, teaching, and themes.

What is God revealing to you?

How can you apply this to your life today?

Prayer + Notes

DAY 25 | MOUNTAINS

Pray over today's scripture, asking the Holy Spirit to lead you. Reread it and write what stands out in the space below.

LUKE 22:39–53

Observe the text for context, teaching, and themes.

What is God revealing to you?

How can you apply this to your life today?

Prayer + Notes

DAY 26 | MOUNTAINS

Pray over today's scripture, asking the Holy Spirit to lead you. Reread it and write what stands out in the space below.

LUKE 23:26–49

Observe the text for context, teaching, and themes.

What is God revealing to you?

How can you apply this to your life today?

Prayer + Notes

DAY 27 | MOUNTAINS

Pray over today's scripture, asking the Holy Spirit to lead you. Reread it and write what stands out in the space below.

MATTHEW 28:16–20

Observe the text for context, teaching, and themes.

What is God revealing to you?

How can you apply this to your life today?

Prayer + Notes

DAY 28 | MOUNTAINS

Pray over today's scripture, asking the Holy Spirit to lead you. Reread it and write what stands out in the space below.

1 CORINTHIANS 13:2

Observe the text for context, teaching, and themes.

What is God revealing to you?

How can you apply this to your life today?

Prayer + Notes

DAY 29 | MOUNTAINS

Pray over today's scripture, asking the Holy Spirit to lead you. Reread it and write what stands out in the space below.

PSALM 121

Observe the text for context, teaching, and themes.

What is God revealing to you?

How can you apply this to your life today?

Prayer + Notes

DAY 30 | MOUNTAINS

Pray over today's scripture, asking the Holy Spirit to lead you. Reread it and write what stands out in the space below.

HEBREWS 12:18–24

Observe the text for context, teaching, and themes.

What is God revealing to you?

How can you apply this to your life today?

Prayer + Notes

insights + action

But prove yourselves doers of the word.

JAMES 1:22a

INSIGHTS | MOUNTAINS

Let's revisit the last 30 days! Consider and meditate on your last 30 days spent in the Word of God and in prayer. Identify key insights about mountains from the Holy Spirit and capture them below.

ACTION | MOUNTAINS

Now let's turn your insights into faith-based action steps!

Draw/write what comes to mind. Be as specific as possible.

> **TIP**: *For a starting point, review your life application notes from days 1–30.*

MOUNTAINS

We are celebrating and praising God for the progress you have made in this journey. Whatever that may look like for you, you did it!

Redefine the full meaning of mountains in your own words, using your newly-gained, biblical insight.

Who can you share this with?

From the end of the
earth I call to You when
my heart is faint;
Lead me to the rock that
is higher than I.

PSALM 61:2

Get your new journal at
hillseedjournals.com

www.ingramcontent.com/pod-product-compliance
Lightning Source LLC
Chambersburg PA
CBHW041309110526
44590CB00028B/4304